Sisterhood is about sharing
the joys of childhood,
the challenges of adulthood,
and a lifetime of love
and friendship.

— NATALIE EVANS

Blue Mountain Arts®

Bestselling Titles

By Susan Polis Schutz:
To My Daughter, with Love, on the Important Things in Life
To My Son with Love

By Douglas Pagels:
30 Beautiful Things That Are True About You
42 Gifts I'd Like to Give to You
100 Things to Always Remember... and One Thing to Never Forget
May You Always Have an Angel by Your Side
To the One Person I Consider to Be My Soul Mate

Is It Time to Make a Change?
by Deanna Beisser

I Prayed for You Today
To the Love of My Life
by Donna Fargo

Anthologies:
Always Believe in Yourself and Your Dreams
For You, My Daughter
Friends for Life
Hang In There
I Love You, Mom
I'm Glad You Are My Sister
The Joys and Challenges of Motherhood
The Language of Recovery
Marriage Is a Promise of Love
Teaching and Learning Are Lifelong Journeys
There Is Greatness Within You, My Son
Think Positive Thoughts Every Day
Thoughts to Share with a Wonderful Teenager
True Wealth
With God by Your Side ...You Never Have to Be Alone
You're Just like a Sister to Me

Sisterhood

A book to honor
everything sisters share...
from **secrets** and **memories**
to laughter and clothes

Edited by Suzanne Moore

Blue Mountain Press™
Boulder, Colorado

Library of Congress Control Number: 2005905275
ISBN: 1-59842-067-4

ACKNOWLEDGMENTS appear on page 64.

Certain trademarks are used under license.
BLUE MOUNTAIN PRESS is registered in U.S. Patent and Trademark Office.

Printed in the United States of America.
First Printing: 2006

 This book is printed on recycled paper.

This book is printed on fine quality, laid embossed, 80 lb. paper. This paper has been specially produced to be acid free (neutral pH) and contains no groundwood or unbleached pulp. It conforms with the requirements of the American National Standards Institute, Inc., so as to ensure that this book will last and be enjoyed by future generations.

Blue Mountain Arts, Inc.

P.O. Box 4549, Boulder, Colorado 80306

CONTENTS

5

Between Sisters

There's something special that sisters share. It's more than memories of bikes and boyfriends, school days and holidays, and the never-ending battle to sit in the front seat. Sisters share stormy nights under the covers and hectic mornings in the bathroom and (oh, so reluctantly) that last little piece of apple pie. They share stock tips and recipes for potato salad and stories about relatives they never met. Most important of all, what sisters share best is their experience of being... sisters.

— RACHEL SNYDER

Of the many relationships in a woman's life, the bond between sisters is unique, stretching and bending through periods of closeness and distance, but almost never breaking. Sisterly ties tend to have fewer emotional knots than the ones that bind mothers and daughters. Sisters are girlfriends, rivals, listening posts, shopping buddies, confidantes, and so much more.

— CAROL SALINE

The love between sisters
has been there for every yesterday —
from baby dolls and stickers
to braces and boys
to real-life babies, careers, and families.
It is a bond that can never be broken.
There may be fights and disagreements,
but they never last long.
There may be tears, but they will always
be washed away by laughter.
The love between sisters
is made up of more than family ties.
It is the best kind of friendship —
the kind that knows every memory
and every bit of history, as well as every
hope and dream for tomorrow.
It is a constant, warm reminder
that there will always be someone
who understands, cares, supports, and loves
with the most unconditional
kind of love in the world...
the love between sisters.

— CAROL THOMAS

When you're little, a sister is...
sharing cookies and a glass of milk,
riding the school bus home together,
playing dolls and dress-up,
arguing over whose turn it is
to set the dinner table,
and swapping your favorite books.

When you're grown up, a sister is...
sharing a cup of coffee
and splitting the muffin (fewer calories!),
driving in the car to Mom's house,
going shopping together for clothes,
watching each other's kids,
arguing over whose turn it is
to have Thanksgiving dinner at her house,
and swapping your favorite books.

My sister and I have both grown up,
but as each year passes by,
I realize that most important of all...
a sister is forever.

— PAULA HOLMES-EBER

A sister's love is like no other. It is history and hope, poetry and reality, challenge and support, laughter and tears. Other loves may come and go, but ours is guaranteed for a lifetime.

— PAMELA KOEHLINGER

Who could say when our solidarity began?... Just as it's impossible to point to the very moment one falls in love, so it was with becoming sisters. An accumulation of shocks of recognition, gradual but irrevocable, until we could not imagine how we had survived before.

— ELIZABETH FISHEL

Sisterhood is not just about sharing genes. It's about sharing jeans and sweaters, hopes and dreams, laughter and tears. It's about sharing the joys of childhood, the challenges of adulthood, and a lifetime of love and friendship.

— NATALIE EVANS

Let's Be Little Sisters Again

Let's build sandcastles
where kings and queens live;
we'll make little windows
with our fingertips.
Let's play dress-up;
you can be the princess,
and I'll wear purple flowers
and bring some tea.
Let's dance in the puddles,
wear yellow galoshes,
taste the rain as it falls
from the sky.
Let's make frosty angels,
bury ourselves in the snow,
and with our make-believe wings
fly far, far away.
Let's forget our responsibilities.
Let's forget that we have grown up.
Let's be little sisters again.

— DIANE MASTROMARINO

Do you remember this place?
I return to it often with thoughts of you
where we sipped tea in pearl necklaces
and high heels too high
We rode on wooden horses
into kingdoms of make-believe
where daisies crowned our heads like halos
and ice-cream cones were our delicacy
With building blocks we touched the sky
until they toppled to the ground
We never had to pick up the pieces alone
We had each other

Some things never change

— LIA BROOKES

A sister is a little bit of childhood
that can never be lost.

— MARION GARRETTY

What It Means to Have a Sister

To have a sister is to know
that no matter how many times
you tell her you don't want to get wet,
she will still push you in.
No matter how many times you say
you don't want to go on the roller coaster,
you'll end up going on it twice.
No matter how many times
you tell her to leave you alone,
she'll pester you ten times more than usual.

To have a sister is to know
that no matter how much
you might want to punch her,
you want to hug her more.
No matter how much she annoys you,
you will always want her around.
No matter how many times she makes you cry,
she makes you smile twice as much.

To have a sister is to know
that no matter how busy she is,
she will always have time for you.
No matter what life gives her,
she will share some with you.
No matter how much of her heart
she gives away,
there will always be a piece for you.

To have a sister is to know
that no matter how sad you feel,
she will always cheer you up.
No matter how many people let you down,
you can count on her.
No matter what life throws at you,
she'll help you catch as much as she can.
No matter how alone you are in the world,
there will always be a place for you
at her dinner table.

— KELLY PULLEN

The Spirit of Sisterhood

I've always been intrigued by the spirit of sisters. I can't tell you how often I've watched two women walking down a street and intuitively, I know they're sisters. There's a certain intimacy that makes them so different from close friends. Sisterhood is such a powerful relationship.

— SHARON J. WOHLMUTH

Sisters function as safety nets in a chaotic world simply by being there for each other. Brothers share the biological link, but they're... just different. They rarely seem as emotionally glued as girls who grew up under the same roof. What sets sisters apart from brothers — and also from friends — is a very intimate meshing of heart, soul, and the mystical cords of memory.

— CAROL SALINE

Sisterhood, both biological and social, is not simply about sharing feelings but involves the revelation of passionate truth, an encouragement to tell those stories buried deep inside.

— PATRICIA FOSTER

I've watched my daughters weave their lives together until they can read each other's thoughts, make each other laugh or cry, finish each other's sentences. Each knows the other thoroughly, historically, wordlessly, back to infancy and up to yesterday....

Writing this, I realize how sweet and slippery is this word "sister" — big enough to stretch beyond biology and across time; flexible enough to define soulmates and virtual strangers; precise enough to embrace me... my two daughters, and all the sisterhoods in between.

— LETTY COTTIN POGREBIN

Sisters stay

When everybody else
　　would turn away,
When circumstances put you
　　at your worst.

Sisters share
Memories of childhood
　　sweet and bitter,
Memories that keep when
　　all else changes.

Sisters hope
For all things good
　　and beautiful and true,
For happiness in family,
　　in work, and in life.

Sisters care
To take the time to listen
　　and to laugh,
To give from hands
　　that are already busy.

Sisters love
To tell their deepest secrets
　　to each other,
To say "I love you..."
　　just as I do now.

— RUTH TAPIO

Top Ten Reasons to Show Appreciation for Your Sister

10. No one can imitate your mother better.

9. You can always count on her in an emergency.

8. No one else can get away with saying, "Those jeans make your butt look huge!"

7. She knows where the silverware drawer should be located.

6. You may need an organ donor one day.

5. She won't let anyone, besides herself, criticize you.

4. She knows how a towel should be folded.

3. She'll take your side — even when you're wrong.

2. Since you are no longer living under the same roof, she can't borrow and ruin your favorite skirt without asking.

1. All sisters turn into their mothers eventually.

— TRICIA ELEOGRAM AND STACEY BERRY

Sisters Share So Much

A sister shares
the memories of yesterday,
the joys of today,
and the hopes of tomorrow.

— AUTHOR UNKNOWN

Here is what parents require of sisters: You must share your playthings, your bedroom, your meals, your bath, your bedtime, your school, your teachers, your rewards, your punishments, your friends, your family... your dog, your computer, your life, liberty, and pursuit of happiness — *all without showing any signs of jealousy, resentment, or envy!*

Here's what children wonder: Are my parents crazy, or what?

— LINDA SUNSHINE

Sisters laugh a lot and are always there for one another. They share secrets and shoes, happiness and heartache. They hold each other's hands and hearts and believe in each other's dreams.

— ELLE MASTRO

The continual sharing, the can't-wait-to-tell-my-sister, is part of the bonding between sisters. It's a relationship that is not to be taken lightly.

— ROBERT STRAND

For a woman the sister is the other most like ourselves of any creature in the world. She is of the same gender and generation, of the same biological and social heritage. We have the same parents; we grew up in the same family, were exposed to the same values, assumptions, patterns of interaction.... There is no other with whom we share so much.

— CHRISTINE DOWNING

As Sisters...

We have memories no one else
    can ever possess
Sharing secrets Mom and Dad never knew
Escaping together to get ice-cream cones
Doing each other's hair, fighting over toys and boys
Knowing each other's thoughts
Afraid of the same things:
    the dark, monsters, growing up

I think of these childhood moments
Whenever I need a smile or a laugh
Whenever the rain falls too hard
But mostly... all the time

The warmth of the nights we cuddled together
Echoes in our phone conversations
And we still share confidences
Mom and Dad could never imagine
Because you are my sister
My memory, my treasure, my soul

— KRISTIN JOHNSON

It's difficult to describe to someone
Who doesn't have a sister
Exactly what a best friend a sister can be.
But you and I share the same memories,
The same family experiences,
The same emotions,
The same losses,
The same joys.
Whenever I need to be reminded of my roots,
Your image comes to mind.
When I want to understand myself better,
I need only think of the moments we shared.
When I want to smile inside,
I simply recall the sound of your laughter.
The magic of that sound
Erases the miles and years that separate us —
We are young children once again,
Running carefree and barefoot through the fields.
Time stands still,
If only for that moment,
And you are here with me
In my thoughts and in my heart.

— VICTORIA GENNARO

Sisters Share Laughter...

Many women told me they can laugh harder with their sisters than they can with friends. Humor lets sisters sail back to childhood, when the adults didn't have a clue what was so funny at the dinner table or behind the closed bedroom door. The private jokes put us on equal ground with our sisters; it is also a tremendous release.

— BARBARA MATHIAS

It's so easy to be jovial around my sister because she knows how to make me laugh — and laugh at myself. She offers me laughter and forgetting. Takes me out of my head. That gives me the extra boost of energy to do the next mile and the next.

— GAIL HENION

...and Sisters Share Tears

Is solace anywhere more comforting
than in the arms of sisters?

— ALICE WALKER

A ministering angel shall my sister be.

— WILLIAM SHAKESPEARE

To help one another is part of the
religion of our sisterhood.

— LOUISA MAY ALCOTT

To this day, I depend on my sisters
for love and guidance.... If we don't help
each other, who will?

— BARBARA MANDRELL

There's No One like a Sister

A sister is a silver lining
when all you see are clouds;
she's the family comedienne
who's always playing the clown.
She is a real original —
someone you know you can trust.
She's a warm and open-hearted friend
full of laughter, smiles,
and memories given and received.
She is always there
to gently nudge you forward;
she is full of strength
and courage.

A sister is a loving hug

that works its wonders

on your soul.

She grabs life by its ribbons

and unties each day as it comes.

She is a ray of sunshine

when you most need it.

She is memories crafted

    from the heart.

She is a blessing to count

and a thousand more to come.

A sister is latté for your spirit,

a little espresso and cappuccino

    for life's journey.

— LINDA E. KNIGHT

Sisters Can Be Each Other's Closest Friend...

Friends can be close, but none so close as one who shares your history, lineage, and legacy.

— ALDA ELLIS

A loyal sister is worth a thousand friends.

— MARIAN EIGERMAN

My confidante, my counselor
mender of broken hearts
and believer in my dreams
My shopping partner
my adviser, my teacher
my mentor, the one who makes me laugh
the one who holds me when I cry
My sister, my very best friend

— ELLE MASTRO

...or Each Other's Worst Enemy

If you don't understand how a woman could both love her sister dearly and want to wring her neck at the same time, then you were probably an only child.

— LINDA SUNSHINE

Sisters and bathrooms are like oil and water. They don't mix.

— TRICIA ELEOGRAM AND STACEY BERRY

Only when we both grew up a little, only when each of us began to find her own resources, the glimmer of her own real strength, was it possible to think about forming a friendship of equals. When we fought, like couples who've lived together for years, we knew the most tender nerve to strike. But when we decided to cooperate, we became a force to reckon with.

— ELIZABETH FISHEL

"A Tale of Two Sisters"

When my sister and I were younger,
we didn't always get along.
We fought over the bathroom, the phone,
   and even boys.
Back then, if someone had told me
she would become one of the most
precious people in my life,
I would have thought they were nuts!
But the truth is, when I look back over the years,
I see she's always been there.
She supported me, shared coffee and talk;
through laughter and tears,
   she was there by my side.
I am truly thankful for all her devotion,
   unending love, and patience.
She is the best sister anyone could have,
   and I am her greatest fan!

— JOANNA LUCY LAIRD

Growing up, my sister was often my rival: fighting over Mom and Dad's attention, who was smarter and who was cuter, over toys, clothes, and friends. We often took each other's presence for granted, sometimes even wishing we didn't have a sister. Still, there were many important lessons we learned from each other. We learned how to share, how to fight and make up, and how to accept our differences. Mostly, we learned how to love each other even when we didn't like each other. I guess you could say we learned what real love is all about.

— ISABELLA MAEDL

Even though the back-seat battles are in the past, our relationship is still tested occasionally by a disagreement or crisis. But we have been strengthened — as individuals and as sisters — by what we have learned from our childhood experiences.

— DALE V. ATKINS

Sisters Share Memories

Sisters are memories of pillow fights, whispered secrets, ice-cream cones, and castles hidden in the clouds. Sisters are memories of running through the sprinklers on a hot summer day, wishing on dandelions, making cookies and licking the spatula clean. Sisters are memories of all the best things in life.

— RACHYL TAYLOR

Some memories are better than anything that can ever happen to one again.

— WILLA CATHER

In the middle of the traffic
and the scurry,
the carpools and appointments,
I glance in my rearview mirror
and remember us,
coloring in the backseat...

Sister memories make me smile.

— BETH ANTHONY

Memories of our childhood
    are forever alive
in the familiar flash of your smile
or the private language of laughter
that only you and I comprehend —
reminding us that no matter
    how much we grow,
you remain my sister
    and my closest confidante.

— M. MCBARRON KESSLER

Our real possession is our memory. In nothing
else are we rich, in nothing else are we poor.

— ALEXANDAR SMITTY

You keep your past by having sisters. As you get
older, they're the only ones who don't get bored if
you talk about your memories.

— DEBORAH MOGGACH

Sister, I Remember...

I recall many years ago when our days were filled with tea parties and dolls — long summer afternoons lying beneath the clouds as a warm summer breeze brushed against our cheeks.

We would giggle, act silly, and dream. In our minds, we created the perfect husbands, well-behaved children, and huge mansions to live in.

At night we'd count the stars, look for the Big and Little Dipper, and wonder why the man in the moon always seemed to wear a smile.

It was those simple moments in time that bonded our hearts and filled us with cherished memories.

— CATHLEEN ZELLER

Remember the wild red raspberries
And the sandbox where we ate dirt?
(Well, maybe where I ate dirt.)
Remember the swing set that took us
To the sky and back?
Remember how we spiraled through our youth?
Warriors of the same house, under the same
Ruler, battling each other beneath an iron sky.
I admired you in hidden glances,
Marveling at the different souls
One womb could deliver.
And I loved you with a fierceness only a
Sister could know.
We accepted each other's flaws and secretly
Admired how oddly different we both were.
SISTER. You are a landmark that exists in the essence
Of me: a blend of thunderstorms over fields of red
Daisies. May you wake in the morning knowing
You are loved, beautifully and completely.

— KYLA AYERS

Sisters Speak a Language All Their Own

If the telephone companies did a study of communication trends, they would probably discover that calls between sisters are a major contributor to their business. Women told me that it didn't matter how little money they had, their long-distance calls to their sisters, domestic or international, were carried on as if they were chatting across the kitchen table. There is indeed a comfortable and comforting language among sisters. We don't have to explain ourselves or even finish our sentences, because so much is understood.

— BARBARA MATHIAS

We share so many memories — both happy and sad — that we don't have to talk a lot to know what the other is thinking. A look, a sigh, a hint of a smile... that's all it usually takes to get across a message that says "I'm glad today," or "I'm sad today... bear with me." It's comfortable and it's comforting not to have to say a lot.

— PATRICIA ZIEMBA

Sisters speak a language that is based on love, not on words. A thousand things can be said through a hug, a smile, or simply a look in each other's eyes. Sisters share the language of two hearts that are closely and intimately bound by friendship, understanding, and caring that never ends.

— NATALIE EVANS

My sister and I call each other frequently; we're keenly aware of the process of each other's lives, the ups and downs of marriage and work, family and health, the yearly decisions about vacations and Christmas. "What's happening?" my sister says when I pick up the phone. On my desk, I have papers to grade, the first page of a story I'm trying to write. I hear her children arguing in the background, then doors slamming, the intimate noises of family life. Yet for the moment I know she's shut them out, focused totally on me. I feel her waiting, her breath drawing me closer.

I sit back in my chair, prop my feet up on the stool. "You just won't believe this," I begin. And I feel the tug of our secret life.

— PATRICIA FOSTER

Sisters Are Bound by Womanhood

She could as likely have been a brother, a Thomas (for the name was all picked out, ready to weave into the family mythology), and I suspect the Thomas who was never born would have altered my vision, too. But Thomas would have never been flesh of my own flesh, never shared the guts of common experience, the dreams, the fears, the mannerisms, the quirks of fate, the primitive bond of blood. What [my sister] and I were to grow into giving each other was the intimate, exhilarating, and spooky knowledge of someone who was utterly like and utterly unlike the other. Our relationship was simple as breath, complex as circulation. She was only the first person I could tell the truth to.

— ELIZABETH FISHEL

I feel there is something unexplored about women that only a woman can explore.

— GEORGIA O'KEEFFE

Whether we are black or white, fat or thin, outgoing or shy, rich or poor, old or young, we are first and foremost female. Our common bond of feminine experience is stronger than any differences. There is something so essential and primordial in women sharing with other women. It seems the most natural thing in the world.

— BJ GALLAGHER

I have been thinking about the nature and the quiet strength of sisterhood. My sisters and I are... the keepers of each other's secrets and protectors of each other's childhood memories. We are givers and receivers of female wisdom and are constantly learning from each other. We are each other's harshest critics and strongest supporters. As sisters, we mirror and define ourselves as women through each other's eyes.

— DEBRA GINSBERG

Sisters Are Similar, yet Different

There is space within sisterhood for likeness and difference, for the subtle differences that challenge and delight; there is space for disappointment — and surprise.

— CHRISTINE DOWNING

The differences between us are dramatic, and yet we are so closely related. Our interests veer in different directions, and yet our wandering paths began on the stairs of the same front porch. And though some say they find a trace of our faces in one another, it is not clearly so.

But there is one thing I do know, deep inside me: You are someone whose qualities I wish I had more of.

— D. SANBORNE

Your sister is your other self. She is your alter ego, your reflection, your foil, your shadow. She can represent both sides of you at the same time, thus throwing you into an emotional tailspin. You are different in detail of how you live your lives, but not in substance. Interchangeably, you go in and out of each other's shadows. She is your hero.

— BARBARA MATHIAS

My sister is not like me; she is *another* who started me on the journey to myself. I see some traits in her that I want to claim as my own and some that I accept as different and distinctly hers. We are both flawed and cannot answer all of one another's needs. Yet the comfort of knowing that our relationship will survive despite the differences and imperfections — that our connection as sisters provides a more accurate picture of ourselves... guides us in all our close connections.

— JANE MERSKY LEDER

"The Miracle of Sisterhood"

We're not always best friends.
We're very different.
We still give each other
    unsolicited advice
and even fight sometimes.
We get too busy to visit;
    we often drift away.
But we always come back...
because we're sisters.

The miracle of sisterhood
is that whatever separates us
has less power over us
than the memories,
experiences, and feelings
of being family.
And these ties welcome us
home to each other's heart.

We are never so separated

    by arguments

that we can't reunite in compromise.

We praise each other's strengths

and use them for our mutual benefit.

Our busy schedules still include

time for nurturing each other.

We're not the same in the way

we raise our children...

but the child in each of us

remembers all the fun times

we had growing up.

Despite our differences,

we come together

to recapture that happiness

and make it part of our

    lives today...

because we are sisters.

— JACQUELINE SCHIFF

Sisters Share Family Ties

Where we love is home,
Home that our feet may leave,
But not our hearts.

— OLIVER WENDELL HOLMES

Whenever we really need to feel especially loved,
befriended, supported, and cared for in the greatest way,
our hearts can turn to the family and find the very best
always waiting for us.

— BARBARA J. HALL

Thank heaven for those who have always known us...
We belong to each other and always shall.

— SARAH ORNE JEWETT

Family is a feeling of forever
without having to say the words.
It's a feeling of love
without needing to explain why.
It lives in the deepest places of the heart —
where memories are kept,
where laughter is free and easy,
where promises are unspoken and never broken.

Sister, nothing could make me feel better
than having you as family.
I know you will always be in my life —
loving me, supporting me,
and sharing all my favorite memories.
With you, there will always be a place
where I'll feel right at home.
We have a connection between us
that nothing can ever change.

— CAROL THOMAS

From a Big Sister's Heart

Little sister, you started off
Demanding a share in everything that
I considered my own:
My room, my toys, my parents.
You wanted to share the
Gifts I got for the holidays
And my birthday,
My party favors and sleepovers;
You always wanted to share my friends,
My stuff, my space, my world.

And then I grew up
And you grew up,
And you still wanted to share:
The game I made on my own
That no one else wanted to play;
Silly secrets, the kind that
Are made special only
When they're shared;
The spinach and broccoli
Off my plate when Mom wasn't looking;
The blame when we
Both did something silly,
And only I got caught.

And now,
Even when we're both adults,
It's still the same story.
You still demand a share
In my fears and my fancies,
Work worries, money anxieties,
And things I wouldn't dream of telling
Another living soul.

Little sister, you taught me
What it is to share
And what it is to receive.
You gave me
Love, joy, togetherness,
Loyalty, support, and friendship.
You gave me more than I could have imagined,
More than I ever thought possible,
Much, much more than my fair share.

— ANANDAM RAVI

From a Little Sister's Eyes

Once upon a time, not so long ago, a baby was born to a proud big sister. The years went by, and the girls grew...

If the little sister feared monsters under the bed, the big sister became the monster slayer. If the little sister feared bullies, the big sister became the ultimate bodyguard. When the little sister feared growing up, the big sister showed her the way. When the little sister needed a place to stay, the big sister became an innkeeper. Whatever the problem, the big sister found the solution.

Perhaps in all this time, the big sister never saw the way the little sister looked at her. Perhaps she was so busy bandaging the little sister's wounds, she never had the time to see how much she was truly admired by her little sister.

Perhaps the little sister never properly took the time to tell her a million thank-you's for all the hurts, spoken and unspoken, that she made well again. Perhaps the big sister doesn't realize how the little sister could have never survived the things she did and become the woman she did without her. Perhaps the big sister doesn't know that the little sister appreciates and celebrates her for the woman she is.

Let me take this opportunity to tell you... I am honored to have a big sister like you. I am so grateful to you for all you have been to me and the roles you have played in my life. All that I am, and all that I will be... I owe to you. I love you.

— AMANDA HALE

Sisters See Each Other like No One Else Can

Family faces are magic mirrors. Looking at people who belong to us, we see the past, present, and future.

— GAIL LUMET BUCKLEY

As siblings we were inextricably bound, even though our connections were loose and frayed.... And each time we met, we discovered to our surprise and dismay how quickly the intensity of childhood feelings reappeared.... No matter how old we got or how often we tried to show another face, reality was filtered through yesterday's memories.

— JANE MERSKY LEDER

When sisters look into each other's eyes and see the mirror reflecting their "core," they really see only the little girls they once were. They do not see the women they have become.

— LAURA TRACY

In her eyes

I am a superhero, a rocket scientist
a ladybug, and a chef

In my eyes she is a firefighter
a ballerina, a veterinarian
and a pony

We see each other through
rose-colored glasses
through childlike eyes
and dandelion wishes
We see each other
for our hopes and dreams
what we could've been
and what we have become

We see each other as women
as caregivers, as listeners
as leaders, as advisers, as workers
as storytellers, as sisters, and friends

— DEANA MARINO

My Sister Is...

My sister is my heart.
She opens doors to rooms
I never knew were there,
Breaks through walls
I don't recall building.
She lights my darkest corners
With the sparkle in her eyes.

My sister is my soul.
She inspires my wearied spirit
To fly on wings of angels.
But while I hold her hand,
My feet never leave the ground.
She stills my deepest fears
With the wisdom of her song.

My sister is my past.
She writes my history.
In her eyes I recognize myself,
Memories only we can share.
She remembers, she forgives,
She accepts me as I am
With tender understanding.

My sister is my future.
She lives within my dreams.
She sees my undiscovered secrets
And believes in me as I stumble.
She walks in step with me,
Her love lighting my way.

My sister is my strength.
She hears the whispered prayers
That I cannot speak.
She helps me find my smile,
Freely giving hers away.
She catches my tears
In her gentle hands.

My sister is like no one else.
She's my most treasured friend,
Filling up the empty spaces,
Healing broken places.
She is my rock, my inspiration.
Though impossible to define,
In a word, she is... my sister.

— LISA LORDEN

Sisters Share the Deepest Kind of Bond

Who else knows every minute, intimate detail of each other's personality and idiosyncrasies? Secrets not dared shared with Mother? Sisterhood is a powerful bond.

— JANET LANESE

The very word "sisters" has come to mean a bond of soulmates who naturally provide love and support.

— BARBARA MATHIAS

My sisters are as constant and familiar as fixed stars in the night sky. They are my geography.

— DEBRA GINSBERG

When two sisters grow up close in age, and in mind, there is a feeling that the two of them are like one. If nothing else, sisters often feel that it is them against the world.

— LINDA SUNSHINE

No one knows better than a sister how we grew up, and who our friends, teachers, and favorite toys were. No one knows better than she the inner workings of our family, our parents' private and public selves. Although as an adult you and your sister may live in very different worlds... you are sharing a strong bond: the source from which you've learned about life.

— DALE V. ATKINS

Invisible threads are the strongest ties.

— FRIEDRICH NIETZSCHE

Sisters Always Carry Each Other in Their Hearts

Whether they live near each other or far apart, sisters walk through life together. They're there for each other no matter what... sharing everything.

Sisters are connected at the heart and in their blood, and their loyalty to one another is permanent. No one can ever break that bond. They don't give up on each other easily. They have the utmost sensitivity and compassion for one another because they were born into the same family.

Sisters aren't afraid to break rules for each other. They defend each other; they take chances for each other. They've cried together and laughed together. They know each other's secrets. They forgive each other when they make mistakes, and they can almost read each other's mind.

Sisters teach each other lessons as they stand by each other in life, and they are there for each other through everything that matters.

No one can ever take the place of a sister.

— DONNA FARGO

Sisters Grow Closer over the Years

Sisters, while they are growing up, tend to be very rivalrous and as young mothers they are given to continual rivalrous comparisons of their several children. But once the children grow older, sisters draw closer together and, often in old age, they become each other's chosen and happy companions. In addition to their shared memories of childhood and of their relationships to each other's children, they share memories of the same home, the same homemaking style, and the same small prejudices about housekeeping that carry the echoes of their mother's voice.

— MARGARET MEAD

As adults, these legacies we carried with us from childhood complemented one another. The differences seemed a wondrous tool for learning and growth. We would compare notes, acknowledge our different paths, and enjoy the present.... The roles of firstborn and last born, of big sister and baby sister, were no longer meaningful. We were two adults who shared the extra blessing of being sisters.

— JANE MERSKY LEDER

There is an ease in our relationship now that has been hammered out and refined by time. In the ebb and flow of days upon days, we are each other's most constant of constants.

— DEBRA GINSBERG

At our best, we indulge each other's quirkiest habits and keep the darkest secrets, cross the country at a moment's notice to sit all night by a hospital bed or be a member of the wedding. We speak a form of shorthand using cryptic words, peculiar timbres, private signals. We can count on a dependable safety net in the world.

— EMILY GWATHMEY AND ELLEN STERN

Sisters hold the key to each other's soul; they grow and change in many ways. Though they may move thousands of miles away from each other, they stay the same and remain close in the truth they know: they are made for each other to care for and love.

— JACQUELINE SCHIFF

"The Discovery"

My sister and I grew up in the same house, but we never shared the closeness I'd heard sisters were supposed to share. We had our moments, of course, of giggling over Dad's jokes at the dinner table, playing together and fighting together, baking cookies and trading stories. But I always felt our age difference kept us apart. We were never on the same page of our childhoods. I was always a few chapters behind, walking in her shadow and sometimes wondering who that person down the hall really was.

Now that we are adults, everything is different. We share things we never shared before. The years between us have faded away, and we're finally on the same page. We talk about our husbands, our homes, our children, our careers. We share dreams and confessions, worries and celebrations. We give each other advice, and sometimes we even follow it. We go shopping together and say, "Try this on, it would look good on you." We laugh about our memories and create new ones every day.

My sister was always my sister, but now she is something more. She is a beautiful woman whose strength and friendship illuminate my life. We are different but similar, like two sides of the same coin. There is no more big sister and little sister. We are just two women, teaching and learning from each other as we make our way.

Sometimes I think how strange it is that my sister and I could be closer now, with so many miles between us, than we were when we lived under the same roof. How is it that distance and time can cause some relationships to fade, while adding color and vibrancy to others? Most days, though, I put those ponderous questions aside and simply enjoy what the two of us have discovered: a bond that is invisible but evident, a love that knows no bounds, and a friendship that grasps the biggest mystery of all... the meaning of forever.

— KATE FIELDS

Sisterhood Is a Lifelong Connection

When we were children,
having a sister meant
I had someone to dream with,
play games, build forts, and have fun with.
As teens, having a sister
meant sharing secrets and the bathroom,
beauty sessions, makeup lessons,
and whispered confidences
about which boys we had crushes on.
In the autumn years of youth,
having a sister meant
growing apart, leaving home,
exchanging high school for higher learning,
and following separate paths and hopes.
Now, as adults,
having a sister means
warm memories, deep friendship,
different lives but similar journeys,
being close as only siblings can be,
and sharing comforts and joys
in all that life brings to pass.

— NICHOL G. FIRESTONE

It occurs to me that one can never grow up with one's sister. In some secret place we remain seven and eight. And yet we are always family, tied by bonds so deep, so invisible.

— PATRICIA FOSTER

We've shared everything, my sister and I.
Even a room
    filled with laughter and tears
    and all our hopes and fears.
We've shared secrets meant
    for no one but us.
Most of all, we've shared happiness.
There are so many wonderful memories
    with many more to come
    as we grow older... together.

— GWENDA ISAAC JENNINGS

Sisters Are Forever

To have a loving relationship with a sister is not simply to have a buddy or confidante — it is to have a soul mate for life.

— VICTORIA SECUNDA

Sisters are sisters for life and regardless of the happy or unfortunate stories, the bond prevails.... Women from the outside often envy sisters as they see how, regardless of their ups and downs, they almost always put their sisters ahead of everything else. Even if sisters are separated physically or emotionally for a time, the closeness still exists. The bonding is that strong, often one of the strongest familial ties.

— DR. ROBIN HIRTZ MELTZER

So many things in this life
change as time passes by
but one thing that will never change
is my love for you, my sister
As the years pass by
we will grow closer and closer
The bond between our hearts
will grow stronger with every
new memory we share
When we are old women
we will talk about our childhood
We will laugh over things we used to cry over
and we will remember the days
when life stretched out before us
like a glittering road to our dreams
We will think of pillow fights, dandelion wishes
and secrets whispered under deep blue skies
We will remember days of shopping, hours of talking
and years of changing — together, always together —
and we will know that forever still has a meaning
as long as we have each other

— CAROL THOMAS

ACKNOWLEDGMENTS

WE GRATEFULLY ACKNOWLEDGE THE PERMISSION GRANTED BY THE FOLLOWING AUTHORS, PUBLISHERS, AND AUTHORS' REPRESENTATIVES TO REPRINT POEMS OR EXCERPTS FROM THEIR PUBLICATIONS.

Rachel Snyder for "There's something special that sisters share." Copyright © 2006 by Rachel Snyder. All rights reserved. Running Press, a division of Perseus Books, Inc., for "Of the many relationships..." and "Sisters function as safety nets..." by Carol Saline, "I've always been intrigued by..." by Sharon J. Wohlmuth, and "It's so easy to be jovial around..." by Gail Henion from SISTERS by Carol Saline. Copyright © 1994 by Carol Saline. All rights reserved. Patricia Foster for "Sisterhood, both biological and...," "My sister and I call each..." and "It occurs to me that one..." from SISTER TO SISTER, published by Random House, Inc. Copyright © 1995 by Patricia Foster. All rights reserved. Paula Holmes-Eber for "When you're little, a sister is...." Copyright © 2006 by Paula Holmes-Eber. All rights reserved. Conari Press, an imprint of Red Wheel/Weiser, for "Who could say when...," "Only when we both grew up...," and "She could as likely have..." from SISTERS by Elizabeth Fishel. Copyright © 1979, 1994, 1997 by Elizabeth Fishel. All rights reserved. And for "Whether we are black or white...." from EVERYTHING I NEED TO KNOW I LEARNED FROM OTHER WOMEN by BJ Gallagher. Copyright © 2002 by BJ Gallagher. All rights reserved. Andrews McMeel Publishing for "Here is what parents require...," "If you don't understand how...," and "When two sisters grow up..." from MOM LOVES ME BEST by Linda Sunshine. Copyright © 1990, 2006 by Linda Sunshine. All rights reserved. Rosenstone/Wender for "I've watched my daughters weave..." from "Sisters and Secrets" by Letty Cottin Pogrebin from SISTER TO SISTER, edited by Patricia Foster, published by Anchor Books. Copyright © 1995 by Letty Cottin Pogrebin. All rights reserved. Ruth Tapio for "Sisters Stay." Copyright © 2006 by Ruth Tapio. All rights reserved. Mustang Publishing Co., Inc., www.mustangpublishing.com, for "Top Ten Reasons to Show Appreciation for Your Sister" and "Sisters and bathrooms are..." from SISTER STORIES: THE SPIRIT OF SISTERHOOD by Tricia Eleogram and Stacey Berry. Copyright © 1998 by the Sister's Day Council. All rights reserved. New Leaf Press for "The continual sharing..." from MOMENTS FOR SISTERS by Robert Strand. Copyright © 1995 by New Leaf Press. All rights reserved. Christine Downing for "For a woman the sister is..." and "There is space within..." from PSYCHE'S SISTERS, published by Harper & Row. Copyright © 1988 by Christine Downing. All rights reserved. Kristin Johnson for "As Sisters...." Copyright © 2006 by Kristin Johnson. All rights reserved. Victoria Gennaro for "It's difficult to describe...." Copyright © 2006 by Victoria Gennaro. All rights reserved. Alice Walker for "Is solace anywhere...." Copyright © 1998 by Alice Walker. All rights reserved. Bantam Books, a division of Random House, Inc., for "To this day, I depend on my sisters..." from GET TO THE HEART by Barbara Mandrell with George Vescey. Copyright © 1990 by Barbara Mandrell. All rights reserved. Linda E. Knight for "There's No One like a Sister." Copyright © 2006 by Linda E. Knight. All rights reserved. Harvest House Publishers, Eugene, OR, for "Friends can be close..." from ALWAYS SISTERS by Alda Ellis. Copyright © 1998 by Alda Ellis. Reprinted by permission. All rights reserved. Joanna Lucy Laird for "A Tale of Two Sisters." Copyright © 2006 by Joanna Lucy Laird. All rights reserved. RLR Associates, Ltd., for "Many women told me they can laugh," "If the telephone..." "Your sister is your other self," and "The very word..." from BETWEEN SISTERS by Barbara Mathias. Copyright © 1992 by Barbara Mathias. All rights reserved. Beth Anthony for "In the middle of the traffic...." Copyright © 2006 by Beth Anthony. All rights reserved. M. McBarron Kessler for "Memories of our childhood...." Copyright © 2006 by M. McBarron Kessler. All rights reserved. William Morrow and Company, Inc., a division of HarperCollins Publishers, for "You keep your past by having..." by Deborah Moggach and "At our best, we indulge..." by Emily Gwathmey and Ellen Stern from SISTER SETS by Emily Gwathmey and Ellen Stern. Copyright © 1977 by Emily Gwathmey and Ellen Stern. All rights reserved. Cathleen Zeller for "I recall many years ago...." Copyright © 2006 by Cathleen Zeller. All rights reserved. Kyla Ayers for "Remember the wild red raspberries?" Copyright © 2006 by Kyla Ayers. All rights reserved. HarperCollins Publishers for "I have been thinking about...," "My sisters are as constant...," and "There is an ease in our relationship..." from ABOUT MY SISTERS by Debra Ginsberg. Copyright © 2004 by Debra Ginsberg. All rights reserved. And for "Sisters, while they are..." from BLACKBERRY WINTER by Margaret Mead. Copyright © 1972 by Margaret Mead. All rights reserved. St. Martin's Press for "My sister is not just like me...," "As siblings we were...," and "As adults, these legacies..." from BROTHERS & SISTERS: HOW THEY SHAPE OUR LIVES by Jane Mersky Leder. Copyright © 1991 by Jane Mersky Leder. All rights reserved. Jacqueline Schiff for "The Miracle of Sisterhood" and "Sisters hold the heart...." Copyright © 2006 by Jacqueline Schiff. All rights reserved. Anandam Ravi for "From a Big Sister's Heart." Copyright © 2006 by Anandam Ravi. All rights reserved. Amanda Hale for "From a Little Sister's Eyes." Copyright © 2006 by Amanda Hale. All rights reserved. Gail Lumet Buckley for "Family faces are magic mirrors." Copyright © 1998 by Gail Lumet Buckley. All rights reserved. Little, Brown and Company, Inc., for "When sisters look into each other's..." from THE SECRET BETWEEN US by Laura Tracy. Copyright © 1991 by Laura Tracy. Reprinted by permission of Little, Brown and Company, Inc. All rights reserved. Lisa Lorden for "My Sister Is...." Copyright © 2006 by Lisa Lorden. All rights reserved. Janet Lanese for "Who else knows every minute..." from SISTERS ARE LIKE SUNSHINE... THEY BRIGHTEN UP OUR DAYS, published by Simon & Schuster, Inc. Copyright © 1998 by Janet Lanese. All rights reserved. Arbor House for "No one knows better than a sister..." from SISTERS by Dr. Dale V. Atkins. Copyright © 1984 by Dale V. Atkins. All rights reserved. PrimaDonna Entertainment Corp. for "Sisters Always Carry Each Other in Their Hearts" by Donna Fargo. Copyright © 2002 by PrimaDonna Entertainment Corp. All rights reserved. Victoria Secunda for "To have a loving relationship...." Copyright © 1998 by Victoria Secunda. All rights reserved. Kensington Publishing Corp. for "Sisters are sisters for life..." by Dr. Robin Hirtz Meltzer from SISTERS: DEVOTED OR DIVIDED by Susan Ripps. Copyright © 1994 by Susan Shapiro Ripps. All rights reserved. A careful effort has been made to trace the ownership of selections used in this anthology in order to obtain permission to reprint copyrighted material and give proper credit to the copyright owners. If any error or omission has occurred, it is completely inadvertent, and we would like to make corrections in future editions provided that written notification is made to the publisher:

BLUE MOUNTAIN ARTS, INC., P.O. Box 4549, Boulder, Colorado 80306.